POWERFUL PHRASES FOR GOOD LEADERS

UNCOVER THE AMAZING SECRETS TO BECOMING A SUCCESSFUL SALESPERSON AND MENTOR IN YOUR ORGANISATION

BY

Jeff Williams

Copyright©2022 Jeff Williams

All Rights Reserved

TABLE OF CONTENTS

INTRODUCTION

CHAPTER ONE

These Expressions Can Assist You with Sounding All the More Impressive at Work

CHAPTER TWO

These Expressions Can Build Your Charisma at Work and Also As a Salesperson

CONCLUSION

INTRODUCTION

Great pioneers invest a decent measure of energy refining their correspondence style. All things considered, great relational abilities are not just among the most popular delicate abilities; they're likewise fundamental for encouraging solid associations with colleagues, being a more powerful mediator, and having the option to propel individuals.

Thus, the words you utilize matter. What's more, basic verbal propensities or spasms can really hinder clear correspondence. Yet, a portion of the things we say can further develop how we are seen too. Saying "sorry" to an extreme and for some unacceptable reasons could sabotage how sure you show up. Moving your reaction from "sorry for the deferral" to "gratitude for your understanding" broadcasts a more uplifting tone, as well. Another model is "yet," which can appear as though you're refusing the mark of the individual with whom you're talking. All things considered, take a stab at subbing "and," which welcomes further discussion. What other correspondence trades might you at any point make to be an all the more impressive communicator? In here, are some proposals for language trades. They may not work in each circumstance. In any case, when utilized properly, they can assist with moving your correspondence to be all the more impressive. There are a couple of force-pressed phrases that anybody can use to steer a discussion. The following are not many that pioneers use to change their groups.

CHAPTER ONE

These Expressions Can Assist You with Sounding All the More Impressive at Work

1. *I'm sorry*

As I said over, this one is strong on the grounds that it's surprising, and it shows both mindfulness and moral obligation. That is not a manager who hopes to toss the fault quicker than a quarterback going to be sacked.

2. *Let me know more*

It's unconditional. It shows interest. It shows listening abilities.

3. What's working?

Particularly great assuming everybody is grumbling. This one pulls together what's positive. You can expand on what's working before you get into what's not.

4. I'm glad for you

It sounds parental and perhaps that is where its power lies. Yet, I've seen this one both as a provider and a recipient. At the point when it's true, it's a strong expression since it is clear and compact.

5. How might I be of help?

I'm frequently amazed at the reaction. It could be that basically offering an ear helps enough, yet frequently there are a couple of particulars that truly have an effect and are not difficult to do.

6. *What are your objectives?*

This might be the objective for the group or the venture. It might likewise be private objectives including vocation desires. Knowing the objective, as expressed by the individual, can alter your viewpoint or point of view.

7. *What's the most widely recognized thing you've heard representatives protesting about?*

Attempt this one. Many will be timid about it and grumble. They would rather not be seen freely as a downer. However, this question permits them to express out loud whatever "others" are thinking, and in that lies the ability to get to what that individual is thinking.

8. *You have my full help.*

Ego booster on the off chance that I heard

one. What a method for ingraining certainty and trust.

9. Allow me to begin by gloating about you and this group

Assuming that is trailed by points of interest that matter, it's a method for reinforcing certainty and backing.

10. If you were in my shoes, what one thing could you do any other way?

This question gets the audience to offer guidance. In the event that it doesn't work immediately, attempt another form: "Let me know a couple of ways I can get better at what I do."

11. What's keeping you up around evening time?

The manager might be up around evening

time pondering a significant hierarchical or key issue. There can be a presumption that everybody is pondering a similar issue. That is not the situation. Pay attention to what others are stressed over and afterward assist them with addressing their difficulties.

12. How is it that we could get quicker and better?

Speed, effectiveness, and quality inquiries are in every case great to pose. Many counseling organizations make millions clarifying some pressing issues, recording the responses from the representatives, and afterward placing them into shiny reports. Why not ask this straightforwardly, set aside time and cash, and begin making a move?

13. Let me know what you're hearing from clients.

Clients are the soul of an association. A decent pioneer is paying attention to clients straightforwardly and conversing with representatives who have a tremendous measure of data about them. Reorienting discussions to what is important to clients is consistently something positive to do.

14. Anything else?

Anything else? It's an inquiry each pioneer needs to figure out how to utilize. At the point when you pose this unassuming inquiry, you don't actually have the foggiest idea where it will go. What's more, that is the point. Asking 'what else' resembles a key to an entryway. You don't have the foggiest idea of what's behind it, however, you're in an ideal situation for inquiring.

15. For what reason would you say you are glad to work here?

One more to turn to protest around — yet

additionally, an expression that permits individuals to discuss individuals or groups. I take bountiful notes since I catch wind of one more worker who helped on a task or remained late to contribute to something. Pioneers need to track down the unrecognized yet truly great individuals and sing about them.

16. Here's how I can help you

As opposed to saying 'I can't' or 'I'm not ready to,' while you're declining a solicitation, center around the positive, Rather attempt, "This is how I can help you." Like that, you've defined a limit with your client or partner about what you're not capable or able to do, but rather you've additionally shown that you're willing to track down a functional arrangement.

17. I'll find out

At the point when you don't know

something, it's normally really smart to express so rather than feign. In any case, assuming you're in an administrative role or managing clients, individuals asking will need more than that from you. Rather than simply disregarding the request, say "I'll find out for you". This gives the individual asking a confirmation that you care to the point of going above and beyond to find the right solution.

18. *Can you . . .*

It's normal to introduce a solicitation with I realize how occupied you are . . . or I would rather not be a nuisance to you . . . Yet that promptly puts you in a difficult situation since you think that you're making a weight. All things being equal, except there isn't an issue and drop this from your language. Simply request what you want and expect that the individual will inform you as to whether the solicitation is excessively and consciously declined.

19. *Let's tackle this*

In a world loaded up with unclear, tentative words, "address" is one that ought to be dropped. I see a ton of speakers say, we will resolve this issue. What's the significance here? That implies they can expound on it, discuss it, and have discourse, correct? However, that doesn't explicitly mean you will tackle that issue or make a move? Rather than saying, We will resolve what is going on . . . attempt words like handle, battle against, or decrease, which convey activity. Different trades to consider that are more significant and definitive:
• Rather than "permitted," attempt empowered or approved
• Rather than "meeting" an objective or assumption, take a stab at achieving or surpassing

- Rather than "responding to" a circumstance, take a stab at answering or tackling

20. I'm happy you like it

For certain individuals, excusing acclaim is an automatic reaction. On the off chance that they get a commendation, they water it somewhere near saying, "It was nothing . . ." or "It very well may be better . . ." Those reactions do not just downplay your work and capacity, however, they are contemptuous of the individual offering the commendation. All things considered, thank the individual really and add, "I'm happy you like it.

21. I Believe I should help

Advising somebody to quiet down is very nearly an assurance that they will do everything except quiet down. All things being equal, have a go at approving the singular's sentiments and guaranteeing them you comprehend. "I can see you are upset, and I need to help" is a superior choice.

22. I'm cheerful I had the option to help

Expressing checks out "the pleasure is all mine" when somebody says thanks to you. In any case, expressing something like "I'm blissful I had the option to help you" is all the more remarkable on the grounds that it has a constructive outcome on the person that you exceeded everyone's expectations to help.

While straightforward changes in language will not tackle all correspondence issues, being more exact and activity situated in your language can have an effect in lucidity and how you're seen.

CHAPTER TWO

Mystique is difficult to characterize. However, when somebody has appeal, it's self-evident. Magnetic sales reps enjoy a critical upper hand over their opposition since possibilities are far likelier to draw in with them, regard their direction, and pay attention to their pitch. One of the most straightforward ways of turning out to be more magnetic is changing your jargon. Though the accompanying expressions are strong in seclusion; use them together and their belongings will be much more grounded.

These Expressions Can Build Your Charisma at Work and Also As a Salesperson

1. Let me know more

Customary deals calls can feel like cross-examinations if you don't watch out. Appealing sales reps keep away from this issue by answering their possibilities with phrases like:

- Let me know more
- I see

These basic, impartial answers show the rep is tuning in and urges the purchaser to open up. They likewise try not to incite the purchaser to give a specific reaction, dissimilar to driving inquiries, for example, Do you imagine that methodology is working?

2. It's like .../It's like ...

There is an explanation essayists depend on likenesses, similitude, and relationships: These gadgets make your pitch more critical and locked in.

See the distinction:

Previously:

Our device helps you find and interface with detached up-and-comers roughly three months before they begin searching for a task.

Later:

Our instrument helps you find and interface with inactive up-and-comers roughly three months before they begin searching for a task. It resembles you're beginning a long-distance race an hour prior to the following racer.

Thinking of an extraordinary interesting expression on the spot is difficult to do, so when you discover some that work, continue to utilize them.

3. No; yes

Charm and certainty remain inseparable. Whenever you're responding to a nearly finished question, battle the desire to over make sense of it: Basically saying "OK" or "no" will cause you to appear to be undeniably more secure with yourself.

Assuming that your possibility needs more data, they'll demand it. This unobtrusively sets you in an influential place. Besides, you'll abstain from meandering aimlessly -- which will in general reduce your Moxy. Here is an illustration of this strategy:
Prospect: "Do you support the Midwest?"
Rep: "Yes."
Prospect: "Extraordinary, what number of conveyance focuses do you have in the area?"
Rep: "Three."

4.   One of my clients ...

Narrating and allure remain inseparable. Individuals are normally most enchanted while they're engrossed in a story, whether it's a Network program, digital recording, film, play, book, or discourse.
That is the reason client contextual analyses have gigantic power in the deals cycle. Use them to rejuvenate the worth of your item

for your possibilities and show them that they are so like its ongoing clients.

Stories from your own experience can likewise amp up your moxy (despite the fact that being mindful so as to keep up with amazing skills).

For instance, on the off chance that the purchaser is battling with his business' finance framework, you could recount the time your previous organization's situation crashed just before charges were expected. Not exclusively will you win validity, you'll spice up the call.

5.   I'm amped up for ...

Appealing individuals show their feelings suddenly and truly.

Others normally get on those sentiments, which causes them to feel nearer to the appealing individual and more open to communicating their own sentiments.

In view of that, share your feelings - - both

good and pessimistic. Whenever you're energetic about a chance for the purchaser, say, I'm amped up for the opportunity you need to do Y...

Furthermore, when they provide you with a daunting piece of information, say, I'm disheartened to hear Z ... or It disturbs me that ...

Simply ensure you don't go excessively far: On the off chance that you're continuously referencing the way in which you feel or professing to feel things you don't, you'll appear to be amateurish or inauthentic.

6. To recap ...

A reiteration is a strong gadget. Obviously, individuals better recall data the more frequently they hear it. Less instinctively, they're additionally likelier to trust it.

On the off chance that you have a particular truth or contention, you truly need to commute home, take a stab at expressing it toward the start and end of your deals call.

7. Envision ...

Utilize speculative circumstances - - particularly ones that place the purchaser up front - - to spellbind and persuade their crowd.

For example, a rep could request that her possibility envision an existence where she meets her targets much more efficiently. He'll promptly need to arrive at this future state - - making him more responsive to her pitch.

Assume, imagine, consider the possibility that ... and imagine are areas of strength for likewise for making a dream in the purchaser's psyche.

8. Extraordinary inquiry, I'm happy you inquired.

A rep with bunches of charm normally invites her possibilities' inquiries. She realizes the more secure the purchaser feels requesting data or explaining a detail, the likelier he is to trust her.

As an additional advantage, this reaction quietly lifts her possibility's self-confidence. Who could do without thinking of a sagacious inquiry?

CONCLUSION

These are only a couple of expressions that pioneers can utilize. Perhaps you'll end up before a room someplace utilizing one. At the point when you do, focus on the youngster who stops in the lobby. The person might be expounding on you twenty years after the fact.

www.ingramcontent.com/pod-product-compliance
Lightning Source LLC
Chambersburg PA
CBHW050328220526
45465CB00005B/2177